People at Work
Treating and Caring for People

Jan Champney   *Photographs by* Chris Fairclough

W
FRANKLIN WATTS
LONDON • SYDNEY

For Megan

First published in 2008 by Franklin Watts
338 Euston Road, London NW1 3BH

Franklin Watts Australia
Level 17/207 Kent Street
Sydney NSW 2000

Editor: Julia Bird
Art Director: Jonathan Hair
Designer: Jane Hawkins
Photography: Chris Fairclough (unless otherwise credited)

Picture credits:
p.4: (left) Shutterstock © C Docken; (right) istockphoto © Andrew Gentry
p.5: (bottom) istockphoto © Chris Schmidt; p.23: istockphoto © Silvia Jansen; p.25: (top)
Shutterstock © Doxa; (bottom) Alamy © Paul Doyle; p.26: Shutterstock © Jamie Wilson; p.27:
(top) View Pictures; p.28: (top) istockphoto © Andrew Gentry; p.28; (bottom) Corbis
© Chuck Savage.

A CIP catalogue record for this book
is available from the British Library

ISBN: 978 0 7496 7819 7

Dewey Classification: 362.1

Printed in China

Franklin Watts is a division of Hachette Children's Books,
an Hachette Livre UK company.

Note to parents and teachers: Every effort has been made by the Publishers to ensure that the
websites on p.31 of this book are suitable for children, that they are of the highest educational
value, and that they contain no inappropriate or offensive material. However, because of the
nature of the Internet, it is impossible to guarantee that the contents of these sites will not be
altered. We strongly advise that Internet access is supervised by a responsible adult.

Contents

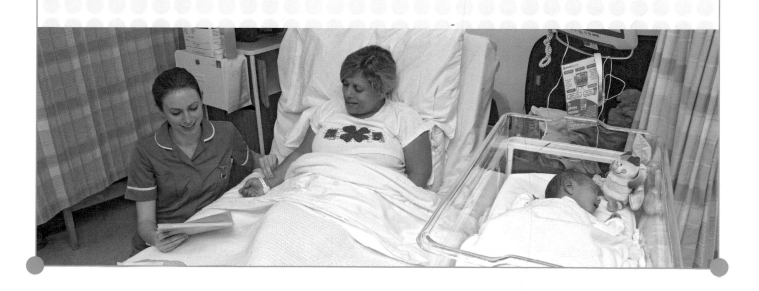

The health sector

We all get ill sometimes. Normally we get better in a few days, but from time to time we might need the help of someone like a doctor or nurse. They are examples of people who work in the **health sector**.

Health sector workers treat people when they are ill or have had an accident. They also help to care for people when they need extra assistance at home.

There are two types of work in the health sector: **medical** and **social care**.

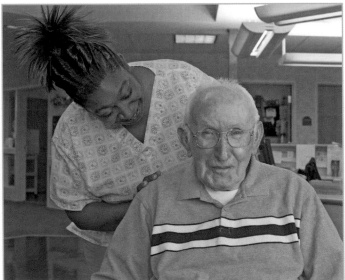

Health sector workers treat both the very young and the very old.

People who work in medical care help people to recover from illness by giving them medicine and performing operations or other treatments. Medical treatment takes place mainly in hospitals, clinics or **surgeries**.

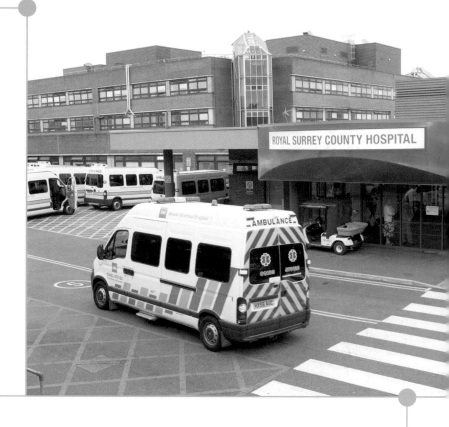

People who need urgent medical care may need to visit a hospital.

Social care work takes place in hospitals, care homes, community centres, children's nurseries or people's own homes. Social work involves caring for people of all ages. It includes helping people to get over their problems by listening to and supporting them. It can also involve helping them with household tasks such as cooking, cleaning and shopping.

Nursery workers are involved in children's social care work.

A visit to the doctor

If you are ill and need some medicine to make you better, you visit your doctor. But first you need to arrange an appointment.

Pauline is a doctors' receptionist. It is her job to make the appointments. She also does office work for the doctors and nurses at the **practice**, answers the telephone and files **patient notes** on her computer.

An important part of the receptionist's job is to make sure patients feel comfortable while they are waiting for an appointment.

Key Questions

What kind of posters are displayed on the walls of your doctor's surgery?

What questions might the doctors' receptionist ask when you or your carer is making an appointment?

If your problem does not seem too serious, you may see a **practice nurse** like Louise instead of a doctor.

Louise says:
"I treat minor illnesses and injuries, give injections, offer general health advice and run **clinics** on things such as asthma and family planning. My day is busy and varied, and never boring!"

In most doctors' surgeries there is also a **community nurse**. He or she can give treatment to patients in their own homes or in the surgery. The community nurse also visits patients who have left hospital and need more help to get better.

Practice nurses are qualified to carry out lots of medical procedures – from first aid to minor operations.

? Key Questions

For what sort of problems might you see a practice nurse rather than a doctor?

Why do you think this is?

Symptoms and treatment

So that the doctor can help, he or she will ask you some questions about the **symptoms** of your illness.

Helena says:
"Every patient is different. I always start off by asking a few simple questions to find out what's wrong, such as if they're in pain and if so where it hurts, or how long they've been feeling ill. When I have some idea of what might be wrong, I often check the patient's temperature, listen to their chest or examine their ears or throat."

When your doctor has found out more about your **condition**, he or she will suggest what treatment you need. This might just be medicine, or it may mean another appointment with a practice or community nurse or a doctor called a **consultant**.

Helena is examining a girl's ear with an instrument called an otoscope.

If the doctor thinks that you need some medicine, he or she will write you a **prescription** which you take to a **pharmacist**. The prescription tells the pharmacist what medicine to give you, how much you need and how often you need to take it.

Tim says:
"I count out the pills and pour medicine into bottles. An important part of my job is giving health advice to customers. I get lots of help from my pharmacy assistant, Kiran. She serves the customers, stocks the shelves and offers information and advice when I'm busy."

Pharmacists usually work in a **pharmacy, laboratory** or hospital. Tim is a pharmacist in a big, busy pharmacy.

Pharmacists need to have a good understanding of science but must also be able to run a business.

At the hospital

If you have a more serious illness or accident, or if you need an operation, you may need to go to hospital.

In every hospital, some people work to care for patients while others help to keep the hospital running. Unlike many workplaces, most people working in a hospital work in day or night **shifts**. This is because people need medical treatment at all times of the day and night.

Level G	(This Floor)
Maternity	SCBU
	Shere Ward
Clinical Investigation	St Catherines Ward
Discharge Lounge	Delivery Suite
Fund Raising	
Level F	
Chilworth Day Unit	Tilford Ward
	Hascombe Childrens' Ward
Onslow Ward	Guildford Clinical Pharmacology
Level B	
Ante Natal Clinic	Maxillo Facial & Orthodontics
Chapel †	Out-patients Dept 1 & 2
Childrens Out-patients	Pharmacy
County Pantry	Physiotherapy
EEG & Respiratory	Rehabilitation & Rheumatology
ENT & Hearing	Toilets
Eye Clinic	Radiology
Fracture Clinic	
Gynaecology	**Way out** - Car Parks & Buses
Level A	
Management Offices	Photography & Graphics
Cashiers Office	Radio Lion
Occupational Health	Restaurant
Social Work Reception	Toilets

Hospitals have different departments to treat different illnesses or parts of the body.

Wards
Each **ward** has nurses to help look after the patients. The type of ward and how long people stay depends on their illness or injury.

Vicky is a senior nurse in the Accident and Emergency Department.

If you have an accident or need emergency treatment, you may be taken to hospital in an ambulance.

? Key Questions

What skills do you think nurses need?

Why do you think nurses and ambulance workers wear a uniform?

Tim says:
"I'm an ambulance worker. I travel to accidents in my ambulance. When I arrive I give any emergency treatment and when the patient is comfortable, I look after him or her during the trip to hospital. When we arrive at the hospital I describe the injuries or illness to the doctor in charge so that the right treatment can be given. If it's an emergency, receiving the proper treatment straightaway can be a matter of life and death. I work very closely with my colleague Karen. We make a good team."

Hospital workers

Hospitals have different types of doctors and nurses to treat the patients.

Doctors and nurses work closely together.

Junior doctors work in hospitals to gain work experience after finishing medical school. They treat patients with the help of more experienced doctors.

Consultants

Consultants are doctors who are experts in one area of medicine. You may need to see one if your illness or injury needs more **specialised** treatment, for example if you have broken a bone or if you need an operation.

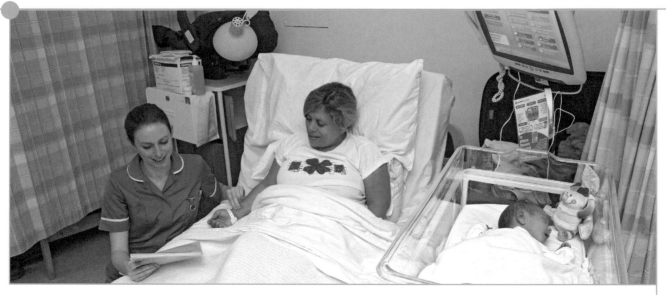

Some hospitals have special **maternity wards** where women go to give birth. The nurses working in these wards are called **midwives**.

Midwives help to look after new mothers and their babies.

? Key Questions

In what ways do you think a midwife can help a new mum?
What skills do midwives need to have?

Steph is a midwife. She says: "Although I do many of the same jobs as other nurses, some aspects of my work are different. As well as looking after babies, I also help the mums before, during and after giving birth. We teach them how to care for their babies. Some midwives visit the new mums and babies when they go home, too."

Behind the scenes

Every hospital has a variety of people working in it. Some employees care for patients, while others help to keep the hospital running.

Healthcare assistants help doctors and nurses with basic patient care. Their tasks include taking temperatures, making beds and helping patients to eat, dress and keep clean.

Operating practitioners keep the **operating theatre** equipment clean before and after an operation. During operations, they pass instruments and dressings to the **surgeon**.

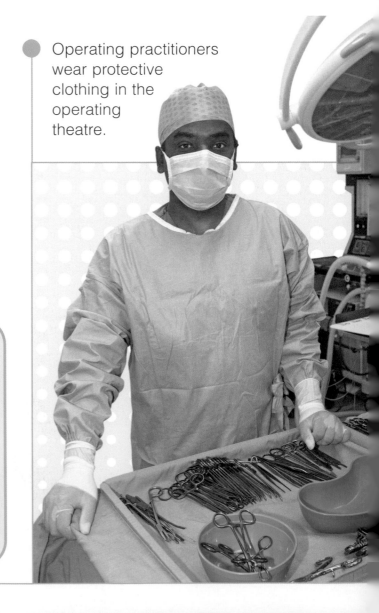

Operating practitioners wear protective clothing in the operating theatre.

Key Questions

Can you think of any other jobs in a hospital that involve supporting the medical workers?

What skills do you need for working in a team?

Radiographer

Woody is a consultant **radiographer** at a hospital. He uses x-rays and other tests to help diagnose and treat patients with a range of illnesses.

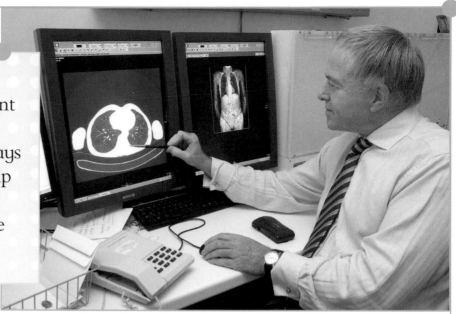

Hospital porters take patients around the hospital by pushing them in a wheelchair or on a trolley. They carry patients' records, medicines and other supplies around the hospital and take samples to the hospital laboratory for testing.

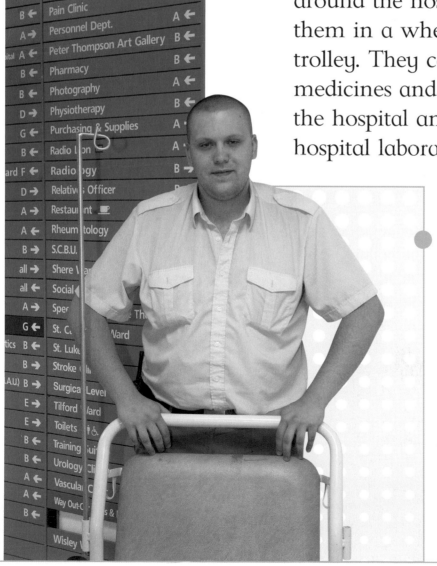

Porters are a key part of any hospital team. They put patients at their ease by talking to them and helping them to get around.

A trip to the dentist

Also working in the health sector are people who specialise in looking after the different parts of the body. These parts include the teeth, eyes, bones, muscles and feet.

Zahir is a dentist. He works in a centre with other dentists and their assistants, called dental nurses. He has worked as a dentist for 15 years.

Zahir says:
"I help my patients to keep their teeth healthy. During a check-up, I might take an x-ray of the patient's teeth and gums. This shows up any problems and tells me if the teeth are healthy. I will then perform any treatment that is needed, such as a filling."

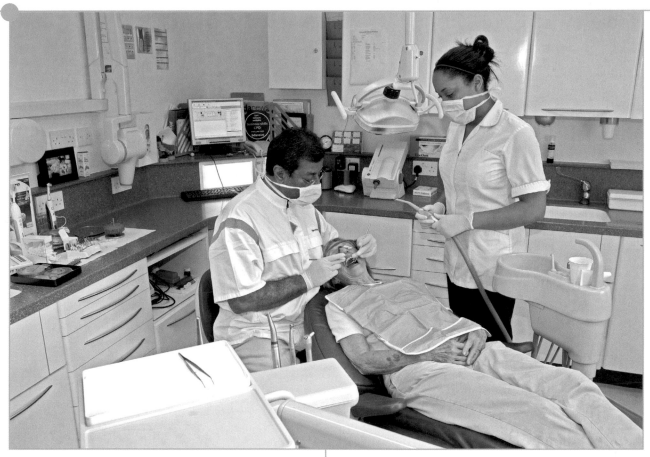

A dental nurse helps the dentist with any procedures.

Dental hygienists work closely with dentists, but are more concerned with cleaning and polishing teeth and looking after gums. They also teach patients about the effects of their diet on their teeth.

Each dentist is helped by a dental nurse. It is the nurse's job to take x-rays, mix fillings and pass instruments to the dentist.

Key Questions

If you were a dentist, what advice would you give to people wanting to take care of their teeth?

Apart from dental skills, what other skills do you think a good dentist might need?

Physiotherapists and podiatrists

Physiotherapists treat a range of problems, such as sports injuries, back problems and sore joints. They also help people to recover after an operation.

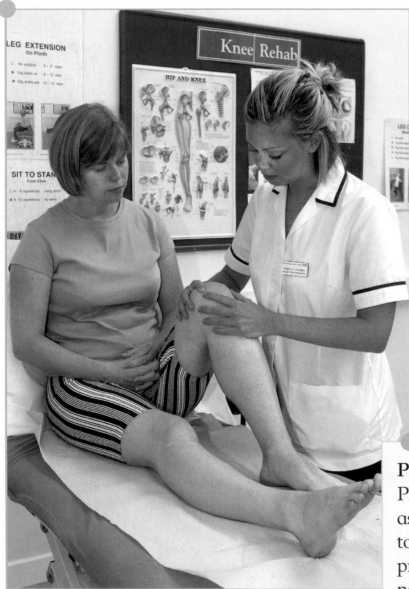

Physiotherapists work in hospitals, local health centres and clinics. Physiotherapists treat patients with their hands or special equipment, and give them gentle exercises to do. In some cases, patients may use a swimming pool. Some physiotherapists specialise in sports or work injuries.

Physiotherapy assistant
Physiotherapists often have an assistant working alongside them to learn 'on the job'. Assistants prepare the equipment and help patients with their exercises.

Podiatrists (also known as chiropodists) look after people's feet. They can work in different places. They visit patients in hospitals, nursing homes and their own homes.

Barbara is a podiatrist. She says: "I trained as a podiatrist at a specialist school for three years. Although I have patients of all ages, many are older people. I look after their feet and toes by treating infections and sore or hard skin. I also watch the way they walk. It is really satisfying to help someone with sore feet become able to walk without pain."

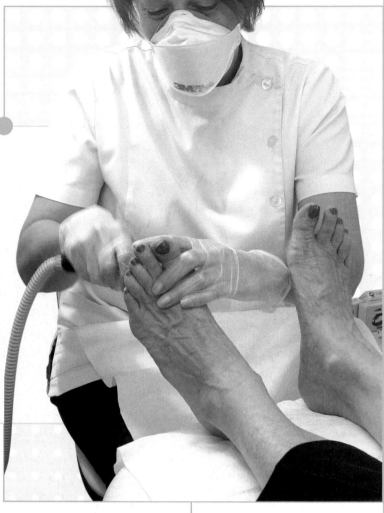

Podiatrists use special equipment to remove hard skin from patients' feet.

? Key Questions

Why do you think a physiotherapist might suggest swimming to help patients get better?

Why do you think podiatrists work in lots of different places?

An appointment with the optometrist

Optometrists, also known as opticians, help to look after people's sight.

Optometrists work in hospitals, health centres and optician shops. They perform tests on the eye to see whether people are suffering from long- or short-sightedness or have any diseases or conditions, such as **diabetes**, that could affect their sight.

This optometrist is checking a patient's sight using an instrument called an opthalmoscope.

Eye tests
An optometrist can tell whether you need to wear glasses or contact glasses by shining torches into your eyes to check how they react to light. He or she will also ask you to read letters from a chart.

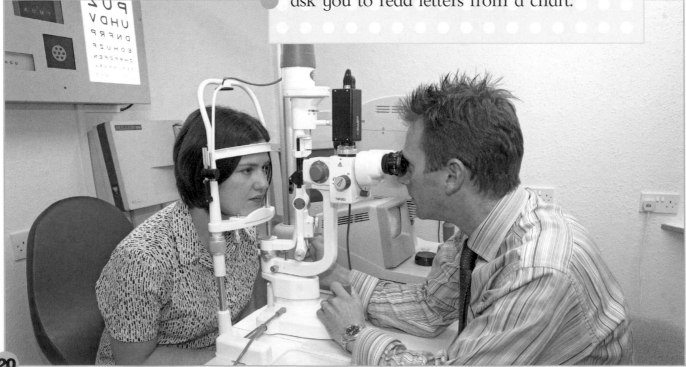

If the optometrist finds there are any medical problems with your sight, you may be sent to a doctor for further treatment. If your sight just needs correcting, the optometrist will work out what strength your glasses or contact lenses need to be.

"Hello, my name is Nigel. I am an optometrist. Some customers come to see me because they are having trouble with their sight. I test their eyes to find out what's wrong and to rule out any more serious conditions, such as **glaucoma** or diabetes. When I've diagnosed the problem, I prescribe the glasses or contact lenses they need. Sometimes I advise them on what frames will suit them."

Social work

The people who work in social care help to keep people happy, healthy and safe.

They work with people of all ages, including children, families and the elderly, helping to solve problems and offering advice and support.

Some aspects of social care jobs are the same as for medical work. Others are different. Here are the main differences:

	Medical	Social care
Places of work	Hospitals, surgeries and clinics	Houses, care homes, centres
What do they do?	Give medicines, do operations and other treatments. Some jobs look at one part of the body	Listen to and visit people at home. Clean, feed and care for people who are old or young. Keep people safe
How old are the people helped?	All ages	All ages. But some jobs specialise in helping certain age groups
When do they help?	Whenever people are ill	Whenever people need extra help

Teamwork
Lots of the people involved in social care work as part of a team. Social work teams can include other medical and social care workers, police officers and teachers.

Social workers can build up strong relationships with the people they help to look after.

Social workers work mainly with people who are going through difficult times in their lives. These can range from family breakdown to drug or alcohol **addiction**, homelessness, on-going physical or learning difficulties or recovery from long-term illness.

Laura is a social worker. She says:
"Every person's or family's needs are different. I spend lots of time talking to people and helping them in the home. My work can take place over a few days or many years. To do this work you really need to enjoy talking and listening to people! Patience and a good sense of humour are really important too."

? Key Questions

Why do you think social workers often work with police officers, teachers and people in medical care?

What do you think are the difficult parts of working in social care?

Supporting people with problems

Some social workers specialise in working with children and young people. Their main responsibility is to help to keep them healthy, safe and happy.

Amanda is a social worker, specialising in children. "I help parents to look after babies, children and teenagers. I get to know families very well so that I can give them the best possible support. Working with young people can be challenging, but it is very rewarding. And it keeps me young too!"

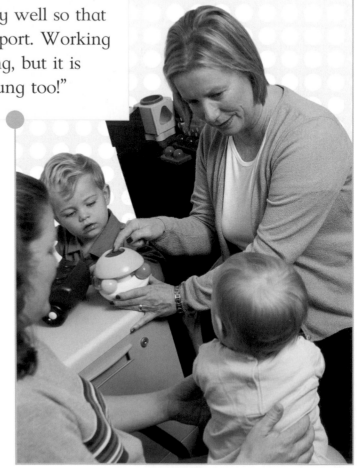

This kind of social work involves lots of talking to the children, their families and other people they know, such as teachers. For example, if a child has a difficult or unhappy home life, a social worker may talk to the school on the family's behalf.

Some social workers help people who are homeless or going through some other kind of crisis. They normally work in a team with police officers and doctors.

Social workers help to provide care and support for people who are living on the streets.

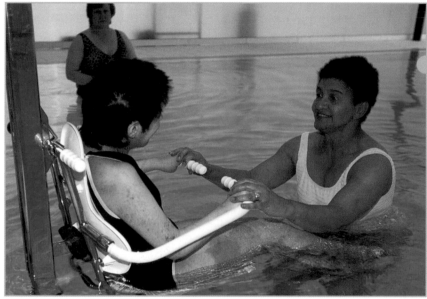

Other social workers work mainly with people who have disabilities, helping them to get around and enjoy activities such as swimming.

Key Questions

What problems do you think social workers help young people with?

What other groups of people might need social care?

Childcare

Lots of parents need help providing care for their children while they are at work. Some of the people who look after children for a living are known as **nannies** and **nursery nurses**.

Susie is a nanny. She cares for two young children while their parents are out at work. She cooks for them, reads with them and plays with them. She also helps to keep the house clean and tidy. Many nannies live with the family they work for.

Susie says:
"I've always wanted to be a nanny because I love being with children. After I left school, I took a course in childcare at a local college. It included work experience with a family, but I also did volunteer work during the holidays. I found a job quite easily after leaving college and I'm very happy with my family. The children can be hard work but they're great fun!"

Nannies can help older children with their reading and writing skills.

Nurseries are usually bright, colourful and friendly.

Nursery nurses also look after young children and babies. They normally work in a nursery, but some also work in schools. They do lots of activities with the children. They paint, read stories, play games and make things with the children.

Henni says:
"I work in a children's nursery with babies, toddlers and young children. We do all sorts of activities to keep the children entertained, including drawing, painting and singing, so it's a busy, fun day. We also make sure the children have a rest during the day - we usually need one too!"

Working with the elderly

When people grow old they may need extra help to look after themselves. Some decide to move into places called **care** (or rest) **homes** so that they can receive greater care.

The people who look after elderly people are called **care assistants**. They help elderly people with things like washing, eating and getting around. They also provide them with companionship.

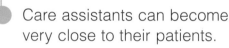
Care assistants can become very close to their patients.

There are always activities in a care home.

Like hospital workers, care assistants often work in shifts and some may even live in the care home where they work.

It is important that care assistants spend time talking to their patients.

Sophie is a care assistant in a care home. "I work in a large house that has lots of rooms where the residents stay. I am part of a team giving them the help that they need, such as washing and getting dressed. I also help to clean their rooms and keep them company. People who are old can become ill and die. When this happens it is very sad and we help the family in any way we can."

Key Questions

What skills do you think care assistants need?

What are the good and bad parts of this work?

What advantages do you think there are to living in a care home?

Glossary

Addiction When a person becomes dependent on a thing such as alcohol or drugs, or an activity, such as gambling.

Care (rest) home A place where old people can live and be looked after.

Community nurse A nurse who works outside a hospital in doctors' surgeries, health centres and people's homes.

Condition State of health.

Consultant A doctor who specialises in a particular illness or part of the body.

Dental hygienist Someone who performs teeth-cleaning treatments and advises patients on how to avoid tooth decay.

Diabetes An illness to do with the blood that can lead to loss of sight.

Glaucoma An eye disease.

Health sector The job family for treating and caring work.

Healthcare assistant Someone who helps people who cannot look after themselves with tasks such as washing, eating and getting dressed.

Laboratory A place where tests and experiments take place.

Maternity ward The department of a hospital that cares for pregnant women and newborn babies.

Medical To do with the practice of medicine.

Midwives Nurses who look after pregnant women and newborn babies.

Nannies People who help to look after the children in a family. Some nannies live with a family, others do not.

Nursery nurses People who work in nurseries with young children.

Operating practitioner Someone who assists with operations in a hospital.

Operating theatre The place in a hospital where operations take place.

Optometrist (optician) Someone who tests people's sight and can prescribe glasses or contact lenses.

Patient notes A record of someone's health.

Pharmacy A place to buy medicine.

Pharmacist Someone who gives out medicine and health advice.

Physiotherapist Someone who treats a range of health problems with special equipment and gentle exercise.

Podiatrist Someone who treats people's feet.

Practice A health centre where you can visit a doctor or nurse.

Practice nurse A nurse who works in a doctors' practice.

Prescription A doctor's written instruction to a pharmacist, telling him or her what kind of medicine and how much of it to give to a patient.

Radiographer Someone who uses computers and reads x-rays to find out what is wrong with a patient.

Shifts Periods of time for which people are at work. In hospitals, many people work day or night shifts.

Social care The job family for helping to care for other people.

Social workers People who work in social care.

Specialise To work in a particular area.

Surgeries Health centres where you can visit a doctor or nurse.

Surgeon A doctor who performs operations.

Symptoms Signs of illness, such as aches and pains or a fever.

Ward A room where people stay when they are in hospital.

Skills and Training

You now know that the health and social care sectors have lots of different jobs on offer.

Many need special skills and training. You can get these skills by going to college or university. However, there are some jobs that can be done with only a small amount of training. Do you want more information on treating and caring? If you do, try these:

Training and qualifications table

Doctor Consultant Junior doctor Pharmacist Dentist Physiotherapist Chiropodist Optometrist Social worker	Degree
Midwife Nurse Operating practitioner Dental hygienist Physiotherapy assistant Nursery nurse	2-3 A-levels NVQ level 3 Level 3 diploma
Practice nurse Paramedic Dental nurse Nanny	4-5 GCSEs (Grades A-C) NVQ level 2 Level 2 diploma
Doctor's receptionist Healthcare assistant Optometrist assistant	GCSEs (Grades D-F) NVQ level 1 Level 1 diploma
Hospital porter Care assistant	Few or no qualifications

The table above shows the normal minimum qualifications needed for each job. There will be times when more or fewer qualifications are needed, so use the table only as a guide!

The qualifications you can take depend on what is on offer in your area. Ask your careers teacher or Connexions PA for advice.

Medical care:

NHS Careers
0845 606 0655
www.nhscareers.nhs.uk

Social care:

Care Commission
0845 6030890
www.carecommission.com

Care Council for Wales/Cyngor Gofal Cymru
029 2022 6257
www.ccwales.org.uk

Childrens Workforce Development Council
01727 738300
www.early-years-nto.org.uk

General Social Care Council
020 7397 5100
www.gscc.org.uk

National Childminding Association
0845 880 0044
www.ncma.org.uk

Northern Ireland Childminding Association
028 9181 1015
www.nicma.org

Northern Ireland Social Care Council
028 9041 7600
www.niscc.info

Scottish Childminding Association
01786 445377
www.childminding.org

Scottish Social Services Council
01382 207101
www.sssc.uk.com

Index